COUNTRY QUILTS

for Friends

18 CHARMING PROJECTS FOR ALL SEASONS

Margaret Peters & Anne Sutton

C&T PUBLISHING

Text © 2004 Margaret Peters and Anne Sutton

Artwork © 2004 C&T Publishing

Publisher: Amy Marson

Editorial Director: Gailen Runge

Editor: Mary Morris

Technical Editor: Karyn Hoyt-Culp, Joyce Lytle

Copyeditor/Proofreader: Eva Erb

Cover Designer: Kristen Yenche

Design Director/Book Designer: Kristen Yenche

Illustrator: Richard Sheppard

Production Assistant: Matt Allen

Quilt Photography by Sharon Reisdorf

Photography: Diane Pedersen, unless otherwise noted

Published by C&T Publishing, Inc., P.O. Box 1456, Lafayette,
   California 94549

Front cover: *It's Christmas Time in the Country*

Back cover: *Honey Bee in the Garden* and *It's Christmas Time in the Country*

Library of Congress Cataloging-in-Publication Data

  Peters, Margaret.

  Country quilts for friends : 18 charming projects for all seasons /
  Margaret Peters and Anne Sutton.

    p. cm.

  Includes bibliographical references.

  ISBN 1-57120-257-9 (paper trade)

  1. Appliqué--Patterns. 2. Quilts. 3. Seasons in art. I. Sutton, Anne.
  II. Title.

  TT779.P484 2004

  746.46'041--dc22

2004002153

10 9 8 7 6 5 4 3 2 1

DEDICATION

This book is dedicated to you . . .
to the friends we know, the ones we
don't know, and the ones we are yet
to meet.

If you've ever had a friend who has
touched your life, or been a friend
who has touched another's life, this
book is written for you.

*A best friend is a sister that
destiny forgot to give you.
Author unknown*

TABLE OF CONTENTS

ACKNOWLEDGMENTS

The dedication is my favorite part of any book and the thing I look for first. As a teacher, you are always hoping to have a student who takes off and flies. That person flew into my life after taking a few classes, and a friendship was born. We have laughed and cried together, enjoying every moment shared; therefore, I dedicate a great portion of this book to Anne Sutton, who puts up with me every day. Thank you for your love and patience, Anne, especially when it comes to computers.

First and foremost, comes my dear husband Pete, who always holds the ladder when I reach for my star. He truly is the wind beneath my wings and the one who gave me four wonderful children Mary, Dianne, Dirk, and Scott. They, in turn, have given us seven cherished grandchildren and six great-grandchildren. To you all, my heartfelt love and gratitude. I love you so.

As always, no book for me is complete without thanking my dear friend Jean Wells. I always say, "God made me an only child because He knew Jean would fill that place when I needed a sister the most." There is no truer friend or sister than Jean.

Also on my list of dear friends who have always been there for me Barbara Brown, Beryl Sue Coulson, Eleanor Broyles, Pearl Maloney, Jeri Hart, and, of course, Alex Anderson.

To the entire C&T staff—my heartfelt thanks go to you. Without your work, none of this would have been done.

Last, but certainly not least, my love and gratitude to Todd and Tony Hensley, whom I have had the great pleasure of watching grow from baseball and soccer players to great businessmen.

Margaret Peters

Thank you to my wonderful family and my husband, Ross. If you're looking for a best friend, just turn and look at your spouse! Ross watched the grandchildren, cooked, cleaned, gardened, and then—when he was too tired to do any more—he gave me much-needed moral support. He was my coach and my counselor all in one.

Thank you to my special friends Anne Bryson and Teresa Adler, who have encouraged me and given their support all along the way.

Thank you to my special quilting group called Wednesday Morning Threads and our wonderful instructor Verna Mosquera. More friendships have sprung from this group than could ever have been expected!

To my wonderful quilter and very special friend, Lynne Todoroff of Walnut Creek, California, my heartfelt gratitude. She moved mountains to get our quilts finished! Thanks Lynne!

Thank you to Todd, Tony, and the entire C&T staff for giving me this opportunity.

Anne Sutton

Thank you to Pat Shaw of Bellingham, Washington, who helped us with a deadline crunch and did the beautiful appliqué on our Honey Bee quilt.

Heartfelt thanks to our dear friend Barbara Brown, who always keeps us laughing.

Now it's time to put on your cozy slippers, get yourself a cup of tea, and sit in your favorite chair while you look through this book. We hope it simply makes you feel good and that it reminds you of all those special friendships you've formed in the quilting world. To all of you who are reading this right now, we say, "Thank You!"

Anne and Margaret

GENERAL INSTRUCTIONS

As our first act of friendship, dear readers, we are going to share our favorite techniques and tips for creating the quilts in this book. All of the projects are sewn with a ¼" seam allowance. Before starting, we suggest that you read through all of the instructions.

STRIP PIECING

It is extremely important to keep cut edges even and use an accurate ¼" seam allowance. Press toward the darker fabric after each piece is sewn, being careful not to stretch the seam. Sometimes a little spray starch will help stabilize the fabric. When joining strips, sew in the opposite direction of the previous strip. This keeps the tensions even and prevents warping.

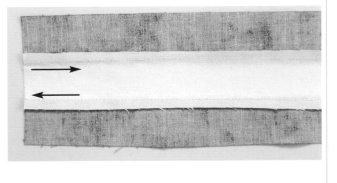

After assembling the strip sets, crosscut segments as directed.

APPLIQUÉ TECHNIQUES
Needle-Turn Appliqué

Trace your appliqué pattern onto the dull side of the freezer paper. Cut on the traced line and iron the shiny side to the right side of your fabric. Use a pencil or pen to trace around the pattern.

Cut ¼" outside the traced line and clip inner curves. Remove the freezer paper.

Put a few tiny drops of glue on the back of the appliqué piece and position on the background fabric. Hold in place with appliqué pins until the glue dots dry.

TIP. *We like to "release" glue as we stitch by pulling very gently on the fabric. This avoids having glued-down spots that show on the front of the appliqué.*

Use a Straw Needle and a single strand of thread to match your appliqué fabric. Holding the appliqué in your nonsewing hand, turn under the seam allowance with the tip of your needle, and hold in place.

With knotted thread, come up from underneath your background fabric, catching the very edge of the appliqué piece.

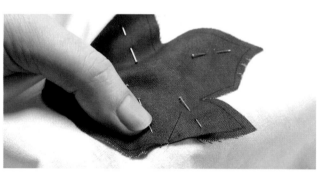

Insert the needle next to where you just came up and back into the background fabric. Come up again ⅛" away and repeat.

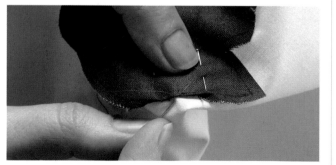

Fusible Webbing Appliqué

It is important to remember to reverse your designs when using fusible webbing. We have already reversed the designs for you. Always buy lightweight fusible webbing for machine stitching.

Fusible webbing has a smooth side and a rough adhesive side. Trace your design on the smooth side of the webbing, cut slightly outside the traced line and place the rough adhesive side down on the wrong side of your fabric. Iron according to manufacturer's directions. Now, cut on the traced line and remove the paper from the back.

TIP. *For ease in removing the paper, score it with a straight pin.*

Place the designs on your background fabric and iron in place. You are ready to blanket stitch!

If you are working with a large design, you can trace the pattern onto the fusible webbing and then cut out the center of the design ¼" inside the traced line.

A friend hears the song in my heart and sings it to me when my memory fails.

Anonymous

Press the design to the wrong side of the background fabric, cut on traced line, and remove paper from back. This method leaves your quilt feeling soft and cuddly.

Appliqué Pressing Sheet

An appliqué pressing sheet will save you hours when working with fusible shapes. Place the appliqué pressing sheet over your master drawing. Place your fused and cutout shapes right side up, directly on top of the sheet, lining up the appliqué with the drawing. Pay attention to what is on top (for example, a hat would be placed over a head). Wherever fabric touches fabric, it will bond together when ironed. With the appliqué pressing sheet, you are able to work in sections and "audition" your fabrics. The sheet holds your designs in place until you are ready to press the entire design together. After pressing your design, let it cool. The completed design can be removed from the sheet intact and is now ready to fuse. Always store your appliqué pressing sheet rolled up. Do not fold or crease.

 If you get glue on your iron, take a fabric softener sheet, scrunch it up, and rub over the bottom of the hot iron. It removes the glue like magic! It also puts a wonderful finish on your iron.

 To protect your ironing board cover, take a piece of freezer paper and iron the shiny side down to the top of your board. You can just peel it off when you are done fusing, and your board is protected.

Spray Starch Method of Appliqué

Trace your pattern onto the dull side of freezer paper using a black permanent pen. With a dry iron, press the shiny side of the traced pattern to the paper side of a second piece of unmarked freezer paper. Cut on the line. Iron this pattern piece, shiny side down, to the wrong side of the fabric. Cut out, leaving a ¼" seam allowance. Press again to secure the pattern to the fabric.

Place over a light box or window and trace any design lines. Clip inside curves. Spray a small amount of spray starch into a small container. Place the pattern piece, fabric side down, on top of the ironing board. Using a small, stiff paintbrush, soak the seam allowance with liquid starch. While still damp, use a toothpick or awl to turn the starched fabric edge onto the pattern and press.

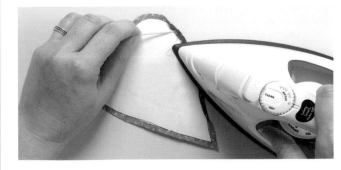

Turn pattern piece over and press lightly. Remove freezer paper while warm. Adhere to background fabric with dots of glue or pins. Appliqué or blanket stitch all edges. We used this method with the pumpkins and leaves in our "When the Frost is on the Pumpkin" quilt (see page 34).

BIAS STRIPS
Bias Bar Method

We suggest you use metal bias bars and not the plastic variety. The width of the bar should be the finished size of your bias strip. Cut your bias strip twice the finished width plus an additional 1". For example, to make a ¼" finished bias strip, you would cut the strip ¼" + ¼" + 1" for a total of 1½". Be very careful not to stretch the bias when cutting and handling.

Fold in half lengthwise, wrong sides together, and press.

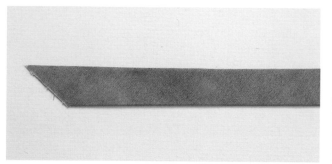

Stitch the length of the bias strip the same distance away from the fold as the finished-sized strip (example: ¼" strip would be stitched ¼" away from folded edge).

Trim the seam allowance very close, leaving not more than ⅛". (The closer you can trim the seam, the better.)

Slip the bias bar into the strip, making sure the seam allowance is centered on the back. Press the seam open. Remove the bias bar and press the strip again.

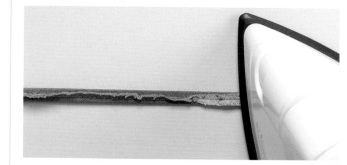

Bias Maker Method

The size of the bias maker you purchase should be the size of your finished bias strip. Cut your bias strip twice the width of your finished bias. Slide the bias strip into the bias maker from the larger end with the wrong side facing up. Using a straight pin, push the bias strip into the bias maker until it protrudes slightly out of the small end.

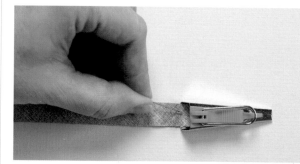

Place the edge of your hot iron onto the fabric and next to the bias maker. Using the handle, pull the bias maker along your fabric strip, pressing as you go. Press the bias strip flat and it is ready to use.

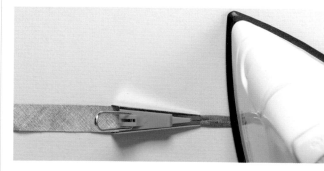

BASIC EMBROIDERY STITCHES

Outline or Stem Stitch

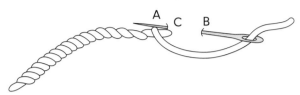

French Knot

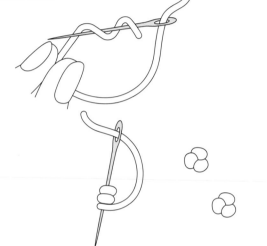

Blanket Stitch

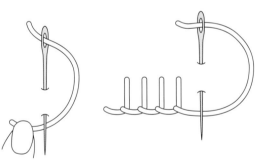

A friend is one who knows you and loves you just the same.

Elbert Hubbard

Lazy Daisy Stitch

Couching

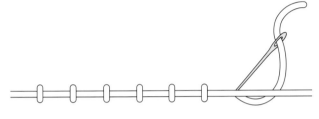

Satin Stitch

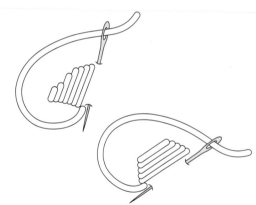

Running Stitch

FINISHING YOUR QUILT

Congratulations! You've finished your quilt top and are now ready to layer your quilt. Measure your quilt top, and cut the backing fabric and the batting 2" larger on all four sides. Now you simply make a quilt "sandwich." Place your backing fabric right side down on a table or the floor. Smooth out any wrinkles. Pull the backing fabric taut and tape it to your work surface with masking tape. Place the batting on top of the backing and smooth out both layers. Place your quilt top right side up on top of the batting. Pin or baste your "sandwich" together. After basting, remove the masking tape, and you are ready to begin quilting!

BINDING YOUR QUILT
Double Fold Continuous Binding

Measure around the entire quilt and cut enough strips to equal that measurement plus 16" extra. Cut binding strips 2¼" wide, cross grain from selvage to selvage. Cut the selvage edges off. Pin the strips right sides together and stitch with diagonal seams to make one binding strip.

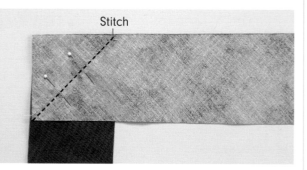

Trim extra fabric from seams, leaving ¼", and press open. Trim the "dog ears."

Fold the strip in half lengthwise with wrong sides together and press. Cut off the excess batting and backing fabric so that all edges are even. Begin in the center of the side of the quilt, leaving a tail of about 8". Match the raw edges of the binding strip to the raw edges of the quilt, right sides together. Stitch to the edge of the quilt with a ¼" seam allowance. Stop ¼" from the corner of the quilt and backstitch.

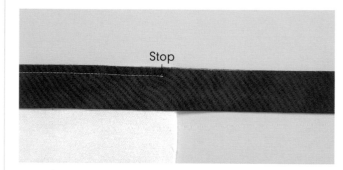

Remove the quilt from the machine and cut threads. Fold the binding strip straight up, making a diagonal fold.

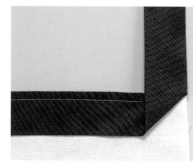

Bring the binding strip down to the next edge of the quilt, keeping the diagonal fold in place.

Start stitching at the corner edge of the quilt and continue until you are ¼" away from the next corner. Repeat for each corner of the quilt, and stitch the binding down until you come to about 4" from where you started stitching. Backstitch and clip your threads. You should have some binding left free.

Finishing the Binding

To finish the binding strip, begin with the quilt facing right side up and the raw edge of the binding facing away from you.

Cut the strip on the right, half way between where you started and stopped stitching.

Place left strip over right strip. Cut left strip 2¼" longer than the right strip. (Cut the same width as your binding.)

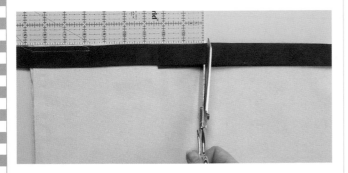

Open the binding strip on the right side. Open the left binding strip and place it perpendicular to the right binding strip, right sides together with raw edges even. Mark and stitch a diagonal seam. Trim the seam to ¼".

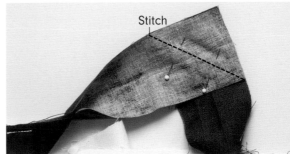

Stitch

Refold the binding, wrong sides together, and finish sewing. Turn the binding to the back of the quilt and hand stitch in place. When you come to a corner, fold into a miter and anchor the corner with a few stitches.

If you want a fast way to finish your binding, fold in the starting end of the binding strip ¼" and start stitching the binding to the edge of the quilt, about 4" away from the end. Continue around the quilt. When you come to about 4" away from where you started, stop stitching. Remove the quilt from the machine and trim the threads. Place the end into the folded starting point of the binding strip. Pin and finish stitching.

Real friends are those who, when you feel you've made a fool of yourself, don't feel you've done a permanent job.

Author unknown.

Chapter One

IT MUST BE SPRING!

Friendships are seeded with thoughtfulness. They grow with a little kindness, and they bloom when nurtured. Be sure, therefore, to take time to enjoy each other!

Things to share with friends…

Tie fresh rosemary sprigs, either from your garden or the market, with a satin ribbon and deliver them to all your friends on the first day of spring. Include a little note thanking them for their friendship.

For those special friends, place some grass and dyed eggs in a tiny sewing basket. What a nice surprise for a dear friend.

Take a walk in the park with a friend who just needs to talk. Sometimes the gift of listening is the best gift you can give. Let the sun shine on your faces, breathe in the spring air, and troubles may disappear for a while.

If you are lucky enough to have a garden, grow a flowering plant for each one of your friends. When the plants bloom, invite your friends over for tea and let them each pick a flower. Provide each friend with a tiny vase tied with a pretty ribbon.

A friendship can weather most things and thrive in thin soil —but it needs a little mulch of letters and phone calls and small silly presents every so often —just to save it from drying out completely.

Pam Brown

HONEY BEE

Finished quilt size: 53" x 53". Appliquéd by Pat Shaw. Quilted by Lynne Todoroff.

While researching old quilt blocks, we came across this long-forgotten block called "Honey Bee." With a name as cute as that, we knew it had to become a springtime quilt. You could easily make this into a bed-size quilt by adding another row and a larger border!

> *Remember that the most valuable antiques are dear old friends.*
>
> *H. Jackson*

MATERIALS

1¾ yards red (this includes ½ yard for binding)

3 yards white

½ yard green

3½ yards backing

57" x 57" batting

CUTTING INSTRUCTIONS

Red: Cut 5 strips 2½" x width of fabric for honey bee blocks.

Cut and piece 2 strips 1½" x width of fabric, then cut 2 borders 1½" x 51½" for sides.

Cut and piece 2 strips 1½" x width of fabric, then cut 2 borders 1½" x 53½" for top and bottom.

Cut 6 strips 2¼" x width of fabric for binding.

White: Cut 5 strips 2½" x width of fabric for honey bee blocks.

Cut 10 strips 3½" x width of fabric, then cut into 36 rectangles 3½" x 6½" and 36 squares 3½" x 3½" for Honey Bee blocks.

Cut 2 strips 12½" x width of fabric, then cut into 4 squares 12½" x 12½" for white alternating blocks.

Cut setting triangles and corner triangles (above right).

> *Scatter seeds of blessing wherever you go and watch your garden of friendship grow.*
>
> *Author unknown*

We have included two methods for cutting setting and corner triangles. Method A will give you exact size triangles. Method B allows you extra fabric, which can be trimmed to size after sewing together the quilt top. Whichever you choose, it is important to remember that both will give you triangles with the outside edge on the straight of the grain.

METHOD A:
Setting triangles: Cut 2 squares 18¼" x 18¼", then cut diagonally in both directions.

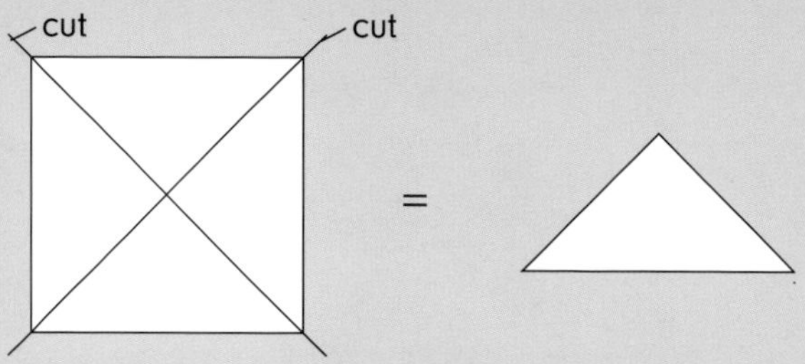

Corner triangles: Cut 2 squares 9⅜" x 9⅜", then cut diagonally in one direction.

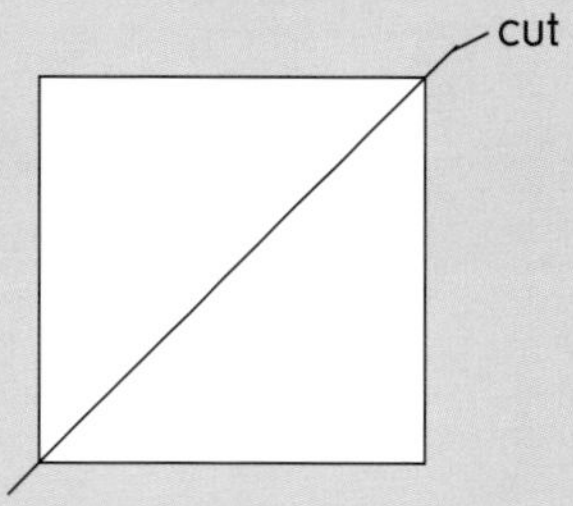

METHOD B:
Setting triangles: Cut 2 squares 20" x 20", then cut diagonally in both directions, as in Method A.

Corner triangles: Cut 2 squares 14" x 14", then cut diagonally in one direction, as in Method A.

Appliqué fabrics: Cut out shapes for your favorite method of appliqué (see General Instructions, pages 5–8), using the patterns on the pullout.

Cut out 36 large red bee bodies.

Cut 72 large green bee wings.

❋ NOW LET'S SEW!
Honey Bee Blocks

1. Sew 1 red 2½" strip to each side of 1 white 2½" strip. Press seams toward red. Make 2. Crosscut into 18 units 2½" x 6 ½".

2. Sew 1 white 2½" strip to each side of 1 red 2½" strip. Press seams toward red. Crosscut into 9 units 2½" x 6½".

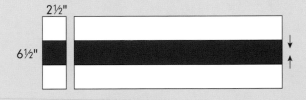

3. Assemble 9 Honey Bee blocks. Press seams in direction of arrows.

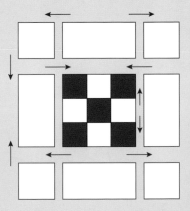

4. Using your favorite method (see General Instructions, pages 5–8), appliqué 4 red bee bodies and 8 green bee wings to each Honey Bee block. Note: Be careful not to pull the appliqué thread too tight. This block has no allowance for shrinkage.

❋ ASSEMBLE THE QUILT

1. Sew the Honey Bee quilt diagonally by rows. Add the 4 corner triangles last. Press. (If using Method B for setting and corner triangles, trim the outside edges to ¼".)

2. Sew side borders to quilt. Press.

3. Sew top and bottom borders to quilt. Press.

4. Your quilt top is now ready to layer and baste (see General Instructions, page 10).

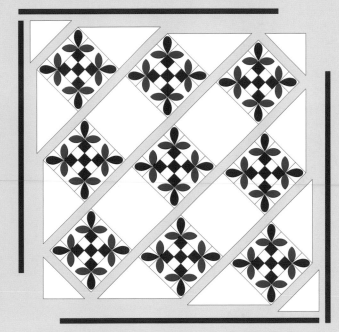

Honey Bee Assembly

5. Quilt as desired.

6. Bind your quilt (see General Instructions, pages 10–11).

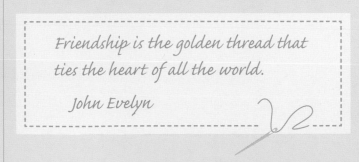

Friendship is the golden thread that ties the heart of all the world.

John Evelyn

HONEY BEE IN THE GARDEN

Finished quilt size: 33"x 39". Quilted by Lynne Todoroff.

A bee flew off of our Honey Bee quilt, and we just had to use him. Here's a wall hanging and pillow to welcome spring, a stuffed bunny, and placemat for Easter!

Flowers of true friendship never fade.

Old Proverb

MATERIALS

¼ yard red print

¼ yard cherry print

⅔ yard center block background

1 fat quarter for bee skep (basket-type bee hive)

2½" x 11" for base of skep

1 fat quarter for bee skep stripes

4" x 4" for bee skep opening

1 fat quarter for rabbit

1 fat quarter for green stem and leaves

8" x 8" for flowers

3" x 3" for flower centers

3" x 3" for flying bee body

5" x 2" for flying bee wings

⅔ yard white

¾ yard green print for wings on Honey Bee blocks and border (also includes ½ yard for binding)

1¼ yards for backing

1 skein #310 black DMC embroidery floss

37" x 43" batting

CUTTING INSTRUCTIONS

Red print: Cut 1 strip 3½" x width of fabric for Four-Patch blocks.

Cut 1 strip 1½" x width of fabric, then cut into 2 rectangles 1½" x 15" and 1 strip 1½" x 9" for Honey Bee blocks.

Cherry print: Cut 1 strip 3½" x width of fabric for Four-Patch blocks.

Center block background: Cut 1 square 18½" x 18½".

White: Cut 2 strips 6½" x width of fabric, then cut into 11 squares 6½" x 6½" for alternating blocks.

Cut 4 strips 2" x width of fabric, then cut into 20 squares 2" x 2", 20 rectangles 2" x 3½", 2 rectangles 1½" x 15", and 1 rectangle 1½" x 9" for Honey Bee blocks.

Green print: Cut 2 strips 2" x 36½" for side borders.

Cut 2 strips 2" x 33½" for top and bottom borders.

Cut 5 strips 2¼" x width of the fabric for binding.

Appliqué fabrics: Cut out shapes for your favorite method of appliqué (see General Instructions, pages 5–8), using the patterns on the pullout.

Cut out 20 small red bee bodies for Honey Bee blocks.

Cut out 40 small green bee wings for Honey Bee blocks.

LET'S START SEWING
Four-Patch Blocks

1. Stitch 1 red print 3½" strip to 1 cherry print 3½" strip. Press seam toward red. Crosscut into 10 units 3½" x 6½".

2. Assemble 9 Four-Patch blocks. Press.

Honey Bee in the Garden   17

Center Block

1. We used needle-turn appliqué to make this quilt (see General Instructions, pages 5–6). Fold the background square in half vertically and finger press. Center bee skep base (bottom of base extends into ¼" seamline) and bee skep over vertical line and pin or glue in place, overlapping base and top.

2. Appliqué base and bee skep. Pin and glue the horizontal strips across the bee skep and appliqué around strips. Follow pattern to place opening.

3. Pin and glue rabbit in place, making sure the foot and paw extend onto bee skep. Pin and glue second ear behind top ear. (Top ear will extend onto side blocks, so you will leave this section free until you have added side blocks and then finish your appliqué.) Appliqué around rabbit. Embroider eye using outline stitch around eye and satin stitch for pupil (see General Instructions, page 9).

4. Make bias flower stems (see General Instructions, page 8). Flower stems are ½" finished bias strips. Cut 1 stem 18½" long and 1 stem 7" long. Following color photo and extending bottom of stem into ¼" seam allowance, pin and glue stem in place, leaving upper right side of stem free until side blocks are attached.

5. Appliqué stem, leaves, and top flower in place. Flying bee and right flower are appliquéd after blocks are attached.

6. Stitch together the top two-thirds of quilt following diagram (see page 19) and press in direction of arrows.

7. Appliqué flying bee body and wings to top edge of center block. Embroider antennae using outline stitch and 2 strands of floss. Add a French knot to top of each antenna.

> *Any day is sunny that's brightened by a smile...Any friendship blossoms if it's tended to with style.*
>
> *Richard Bach*

Honey Bee Blocks

1. Stitch 1 red print 1½" x 15" strip to each side of 1 white 1½" x 15" strip. Press seams toward red. Crosscut into 10 units 1½" x 3½".

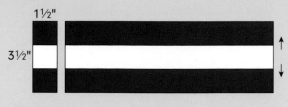

2. Stitch 1 white strip 1½" x 9" to each side of 1 red print strip ½" x 9". Press seams toward red. Crosscut into 5 units 1½" x 3½".

3. Assemble 5 Honey Bee blocks. Press seams in direction of arrows.

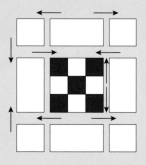

4. Using your favorite method (see General Instructions, pages 5–8), appliqué 4 red bee bodies and 8 green bee wings to each Honey Bee block following the Quilt Schematic on page 19.

ASSEMBLE THE QUILT

1. Sew 2 rows of Honey Bee blocks together. Stitch to top two-thirds of quilt. Press.

2. Add the borders (sides, then top and bottom). Press.

3. Layer and baste your finished quilt top (see General Instructions, page 10).

4. Quilt as desired.

5. Bind your quilt (see General Instructions, pages 10-11).

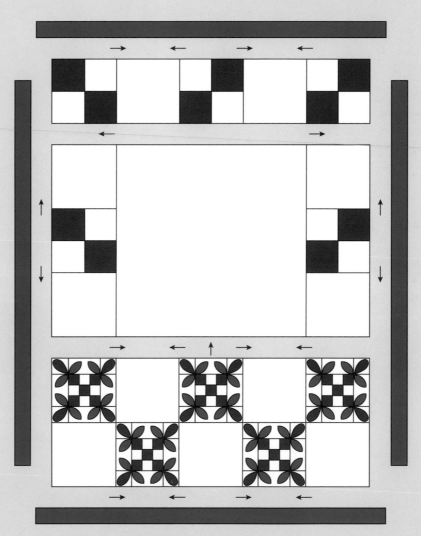

Honey Bee in the Garden Assembly

STUFFED FELT
EASTER BUNNY

Finished bunny size: 15" tall

MATERIALS

26" x 20" wool or wool felt for bunny body, legs, and ears, 6" x 6" contrast wool or wool felt for inside ear

1 skein of each color DMC Embroidery floss #433 for eye, #368 for flower stems, #3746 for flowers, and #3833 for flower centers

1 bag stuffing

Two 5/8" buttons

3" doll needle

Heavy thread (we used linen, but button thread would also work well)

Water erasable marker or iron-on transfer pencil

CONSTRUCTION

1. Cut out bunny fabric as directed on pullout pattern.

2. Trace flower pattern onto bunny front using the iron-on transfer pencil. Follow the manufacturer's directions. If you allow yourself to be the artist you really are, it is easy to draw the design freehand using a water erasable marker. Just draw lines for the stems and flower petals.

3. Using 3 strands of floss, embroider stems using outline stitch, leaves using satin stitch, and flower petals using lazy daisy stitch. Flower centers are French knots. Directions for these stitches can be found in the General Instructions on page 9.

4. Stitch ears, right sides together, and turn. Pin ears to bunny front following placement lines on pattern. Stitch bunny, right sides together, catching raw edge of ears into seam and leaving opening in bunny for stuffing. Clip curves. Turn right-side out and stuff firmly. Stitch opening closed. Embroider eye after stuffing, and pull thread between sides to create a small indentation.

5. Stitch legs, right sides together, leaving an opening for stuffing. Clip curves. Turn right side out and stuff. Stitch opening closed. Attach legs using buttons, heavy thread, and a doll needle. Start from the back of the leg and come up through the hole in the button. Go down through the button, leg, and body. Attach second leg and come up through the second button. Repeat several times to anchor buttons and legs. Tie off thread behind 1 button.

6. Using a running stitch, sew 1/4" from edge. Pull thread tight and stuff tail. Tie off thread and sew tail to body.

True friendship is a plant of slow growth.
George Washington

FELT
BUNNY PILLOW

Finished pillow size: 14" x 18"

■ MATERIALS

½ yard felt for background

¼ yard felt for border

8" x 15" felt for rabbit

2 contrast felt squares 5" x 5" for flower

¼ yard felt for stem and petals

Felt scrap for bee and wings

12" x 16" pillow form

1 novelty button for flower center

1 tiny button for bunny eye

DMC embroidery floss to match fabrics for hand blanket stitch, or thread to match fabric for machine blanket stitch

Freezer paper

■ CUTTING INSTRUCTIONS

Cut 2 rectangles 12½" x 16½" for background and backing.

Cut 4 strips 1½" x 16½" for side borders.

Cut 4 strips 1½" x 14½" for top and bottom borders.

■ CONSTRUCTION

1. Use the patterns on pullout to trace the bunny, stem, flower, and bee onto freezer paper. Press to felt with warm iron. Cut appliqué pieces from felt on traced pattern lines. Remove freezer paper, and center pieces on background fabric. Pin in place.

2. Hand or machine blanket stitch around rabbit, ears, stem, flower, bee wings and bee body. The leaves are gathered in the center with a running stitch and tacked to the stem as shown in the color photo. The stripes on the bee body are done using the outline stitch and 3 strands of floss. Draw antenae onto background following the pattern. Add French knots at the end of each bee antenna.

3. Stitch border strips to background and backing (sides first, then top and bottom).

4. With right sides together, stitch around **outside of border** pillow with ¼" seam leaving opening at bottom for turning.

5. Turn and press the seam. Leave opening at the bottom and stitch in-the-ditch between border and background. Insert pillow form and continue stitching in-the-ditch. Slip stitch opening on outside edge of pillow.

Chapter Two

SUMMER, GLORIOUS SUMMER!

Things to share with friends…

Collect seashells on your vacation and carefully pack them in your luggage for your best friend. Put them in an old canning jar with shells glued on the top, just to let her know you thought about her while you were gone. She can place them in her sewing room, and she'll remember your friendship each time she sees them. Maybe the colors of the shells will inspire her next quilt!

A vase full of flowers, picked fresh from your garden or purchased, is a sure way to perk up a friendship. Place the vase in the center of a fat quarter, gather the fat quarter around the vase and tie it with a string at the top. Nothing else needs to be said, because flowers say it all. Flowers mean as much when they come from a friend as when they come from the love of your life!

Sharing a birdhouse with your fluttering friends is a way of thanking Mother Nature. Put a birdhouse in your garden and, when your feathered friends start a family, you will be rewarded over and over. Friendship is not just about the people in our lives. It's also about our animal friends!

Never lose your little girl heart. Make a batch of cookies and a big pitcher of lemonade. Get your kids, grandkids, or the neighborhood kids and set up a lemonade stand. You will make new friends and supply a memory the children will never forget.

HERE COMES
THE PARADE

Finished quilt size: 42" x 42½". Quilted by Lynne Todoroff.

What's more American than apple pie? A big red barn and farm animals! Put them on parade, and you have a Fourth of July quilt you can make in a weekend and hang . The blue sashing is an optical illusion. The blue is simply part of the Log Cabin block! It sure fooled us!

> *A true friend is the best possession.*
>
> *Benjamin Franklin*

MATERIALS

Log Cabin Blocks:

¼ yard for center squares

3 light fabrics in a range of values: light #1: ¼ yard, medium #2: ¼ yard, and dark #3: ⅓ yard

3 dark fabrics in a range of values: light #4: ¼ yard, medium #5: ⅓ yard, and dark #6: ⅜ yard

Barn and Animal Appliqué Blocks:

¼ yard for animal background (we used the same fabric as dark #6, above)

1 fat quarter for barn roof and door

1 fat quarter for barn front

8" x 8" for sky

2½" x 2½" for star

Assorted 5" x 5" squares for animals

½ yard for sashing strip and border

½ yard for binding

1¾ yards for backing

½ yard light fusible web

1 skein each DMC embroidery floss blanc and #310 black

2 yards ¼"-wide grosgrain ribbon for couching

46" x 47" batting

CUTTING INSTRUCTIONS
Log Cabin Blocks

Note: Once the strips are cut into sections, stack them by letter into piles and label with sticky notes. Arrange stacks in the order they will be used.

A: Center: Cut 2 strips 2" x width of fabric, then cut into 28 squares 2" x 2".

B and C: From light #1, cut 4 strips 1¼" x width of fabric, then cut into 28 rectangles 1¼" x 2" for B, and 28 rectangles 1¼" x 2¾" for C.

D and E: From dark #4, cut 5 strips 1¼" x width of fabric, then cut into 28 rectangles 1¼" x 2¾" for D, and 28 rectangles 1¼" x 3½" for E.

F and G: From light #2, cut 6 strips 1¼" x width of fabric, then cut into 28 rectangles 1¼" x 3½" for F, and 28 rectangles 1¼" x 4¼" for G.

H and I: From dark #5, cut 7 strips 1¼" x width of fabric, then cut into 28 rectangles 1¼" x 4¼" for H, and 28 rectangles 1¼" x 5" for I.

J and K: From light #3, cut 8 strips 1¼" x width of fabric, then cut into 28 rectangles 1¼" x 5" for J, and 28 rectangles 1¼" x 5¾" for K.

L and M: From dark #6, cut 10 strips 1¼" x width of fabric, then cut into 28 rectangles 1¼" x 5¾" for L, and 28 rectangles 1¼" x 6½" for M.

Barn and Animal Appliqué Blocks:

Cut 2 rectangles 1" x 4½" and 1 square 2⅞" x 2⅞" for sky.

Cut 1 square 2⅞" x 2⅞" and 1 rectangle 2½" x 8½" for roof.

Cut 1 rectangle 1½" x 11½" and 2 rectangles 3½" x 4" for barn front.

Cut 2 rectangles 2½" x 3½" for doors.

Cut 1 strip 6½" x 36½" for animal background.

Cut out animal shapes for your favorite method of appliqué, using the patterns on pullout.

Cut 1 strip 1½" x 36½" for sashing.

Cut 2 strips 3½" x 37½" for side borders.

Cut 2 strips 3½" x 42½" for top and bottom borders.

Cut 5 strips 2¼" x width of fabric for binding.

START STITCHING!

Log Cabin Blocks

1. Chain stitch section A to section B with right sides together. (Chain stitch means to feed your pieces of fabric through the machine one after another without lifting the presser foot.) Clip thread between pairs, and press seams away from center squares.

2. Chain stitch section C to AB unit with right sides together. Clip threads between pairs, and press seam away from center block.

3. Chain stitch section D to ABC unit and repeat above process.

4. Chain stitch section E to ABCD unit and repeat above process.

5. You have now gone around the center square on all sides. Continue, adding F, G, H, I J, K, L, and M using the method above. Hint: When sewing Log Cabin blocks, it is sometimes difficult to remember which side you are sewing on. Always stack your blocks so that the piece you just added is on the bottom. The next strip is attached on the right.

6. Make 28 Log Cabin blocks.

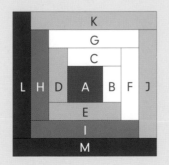

Log Cabin block

Barn and Animal Appliqué Blocks

1. Sew the 2 barn doors together lengthwise. Press seam. Sew 1 barn front to each side of this unit. Press seams. Sew barn top to barn front unit. Press seams.

2. Sew sky #1 to each side of barn front unit. Press seams.

3. Place 1 square each of roof and sky fabric right sides together. Following the diagram below, draw a diagonal line from corner to corner. Stitch ¼" on each side of line. Cut on drawn line. Press seams and clip off corner tails.

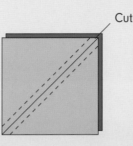

4. Sew 1 sky/roof section to each side of roof #2. Press seams.

5. Sew roof section to barn unit. Press seams.

6. Trace and then fuse animals to background fabric and star to barn roof (see General Instructions, pages 6–7). Patterns are already reversed for tracing.

7. Blanket stitch by hand or machine around all the animals and the star. Add details to animals by embroidering French knots for eyes and using outline stitch for cat's whiskers. Embroider lines on barn door with outline stitch. The couched ribbon joining animals is added after the quilting is done.

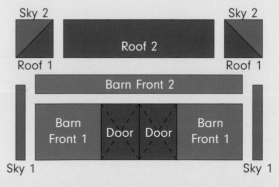

Barn block construction

ASSEMBLE THE QUILT

1. Following the diagram, stitch rows of Log Cabin blocks and the center Barn block together as shown. Press seams in direction of arrows.

2. Attach 1¼" sashing strip to bottom of quilt.

3. Sew 6½" animal strip to bottom of quilt.

4. Add the borders (sides, then top and bottom).

5. You've arrived! Layer and baste, following General Instructions on page 10!

6. Quilt as desired.

7. Couching: Fold end of ribbon under ¼" and tack to rooster's beak. Following color photo and twisting occasionally for whimsy, couch ribbon in place. Turn under end of ribbon ¼" and attach to crow on turtle's back. With remaining ribbon, tie a few bows and attach to the animals of your choice.

8. Bind the quilt (see General Instructions, pages 10–11).

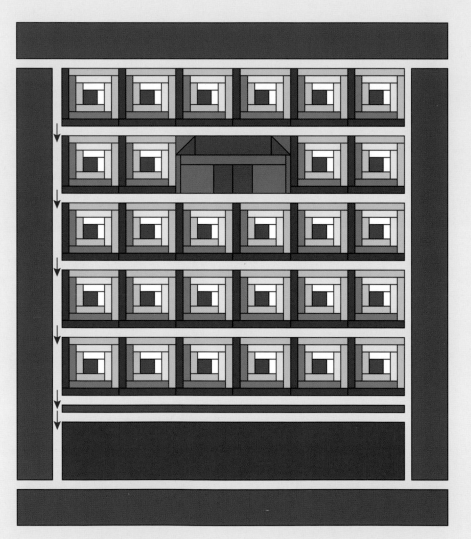

Here Comes the Parade Assembly

JULY 4TH
REDWORK LAMB

Finished redwork size: 12" x 12"

Ah, how good it feels!
The hand of an old friend.

Henry Wadsworth Longfellow

MATERIALS

15½" x 15½" background fabric

15½" x 15½" Quilter's Dream Cotton Request Batting

2 skeins DMC embroidery floss #321 Red

Picture frame with 12" x 12" opening (If your picture frame measures more than 13" x 13" on the outside edges, you will need to add to your cut fabric dimensions. Your fabric should measure 3" larger than the outside edge of the frame.)

Water-soluble fabric marker

Cardboard, cut to fit in picture frame

CONSTRUCTION

1. Using a light box or window, center and trace pattern from pullout onto background fabric with a water-soluble marker.

2. Place batting behind background fabric and embroider the design through both layers with an outline stitch using 2 strands of embroidery floss. Fill in the star with French knots.

3. Centering the redwork over the cardboard, fold the fabric to the back, and tape it in place. Place it in the frame, and you're done!

REVERSIBLE PLACEMATS
FOR SPRING AND SUMMER

Finished placemat size: 19" x 15"

Reverse side of placemat

MATERIALS

½ yard each of 2 contrasting colors of wool felt for each placemat

Scraps of felt for selected designs in the colors of your choice

DMC embroidery floss for hand blanket stitch to match or contrast with your selected felt

Roxanne's Glue-Baste-It (See Resources page 56)

Freezer paper

A friend is like a piece of pie. You never have too many, and they make you happy when you're sad!

Author unknown

CONSTRUCTION

1. Cut 1 rectangle of wool felt 16" x 20". (Trim to 15" x 19" after finishing appliqué.)

2. Use the bunny and bee pattern on pullout for Spring. Trace appliqué patterns onto freezer paper and iron to selected pieces of felt. Cut felt on pattern lines and remove freezer paper. The reverse side of the placemat for July 4th uses the original star and animal patterns on pullout.

3. Following color photos, glue or pin designs to placemat backgrounds. Blanket stitch around designs. The eyes for the rabbit, goose, and pig are French knots. Bee's antennae ends are also French knots. Embroider all remaining details using outline stitch and 2 strands of floss.

4. Place finished sections with wrong sides together and hand blanket stitch around border to create your reversible mat.

SUNBONNETS IN THE USA

Finished quilt size: 48" x 63". Quilted by Lynne Todoroff.

Calling all embroidery machine owners! This quilt was designed for you. We used Betty Alderman's design from Bernina's "United We Stand" embroidery card. You can substitute any design card that uses the outline stitch or any redwork embroidery pattern you like.

Make sure your design will fit into the 6" x 6" finished center square.

MATERIALS

3½ yards white

1½ yards red (includes ½ yard for binding)

Embroidery stabilizer

Machine embroidery thread

3 yards backing

52" x 67" batting

CUTTING INSTRUCTIONS

White: Cut 3 strips 10" x width of fabric, then cut into 12 squares 10" x 10" for center blocks. (They will be trimmed to 6½" x 6½" squares after embroidery.)

Cut 8 strips 2½" x width of fabric for a Puss in the Corner blocks.

Cut 15 strips 1½" x width of fabric for Nine-Patches.

Cut 11 strips 3½" x width of fabric, then cut into 31 rectangles 3½" x 12½" for sashing.

Red: Cut 20 strips 1½" x width of fabric for unit A and Nine-Patches and Puss in the Corner blocks.

Cut 7 strips 2¼" x width of fabric for binding.

NOW LETS SEW!

Machine embroider the 10" x 10" blocks with design of your choice following the manufacturer's directions for your machine. Be sure to stabilize the fabric. Remove the stabilizer from the finished embroidery and trim the blocks to 6½" x 6½".

Nine-Patch Blocks

1. Sew 1 white 1½" strip to each side of 1 red 1½" strip. Press seams toward red strip. Make 6. Crosscut into 136 units, each 1½" x 3½".

2. Sew 1 red 1½" strip to each side of 1 white 1½" strip. Press seams toward red strips. Make 3. Crosscut into 68 units, each 1½" x 3½".

3. Assemble 68 Nine-Patch blocks. Press seams in direction of arrows.

Puss in the Corner blocks

1. Sew 1 red 1½" strip to 1 white 2½" strip. Press seam toward red. Make 8. Crosscut into 48 units, each 3½" x 6½".

2. Assemble 12 Puss in the Corner blocks. Press seams in direction of arrows.

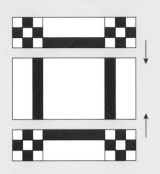

Sashing

Sew 4 Nine-Patch blocks alternating with 3 sashing 3½" x 12½" rectangles. Press toward the rectangles. Make 5.

ASSEMBLE THE QUILT

1. To assemble the blocks in the quilt, lay them out in rows with sashing strips in between. Refer to diagram and photograph.

2. Stitch the blocks together across each row and join the rows to one another in order. Press the top.

3. Your quilt is now ready to layer and baste (see General Instructions, page 10).

4. Quilt as desired.

5. Bind your quilt (see General Instructions, pages 10–11).

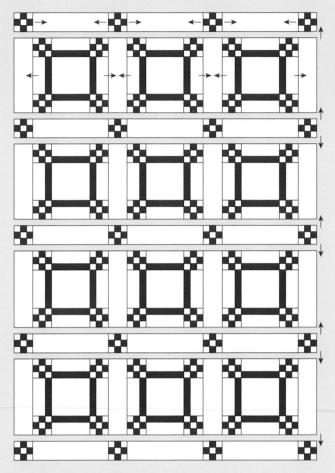

Sunbonnets in the USA Assembly

Friendship with oneself is all-important because without it one cannot be friends with anyone else in the world.

Eleanor Roosevelt

SUNBONNETS IN THE
USA PILLOW

Finished pillow size: 15" x 15". Embroidery done by Sarah Coulson.

We used Betty Alderman's design from Bernina's "Redwork for Children" embroidery card.

 MATERIALS

⅝ yard white

⅛ yard red

½ yard backing

Embroidery stabilizer

Embroidery thread

14" x 14" pillow form

1 package Wrights Maxi Piping

CUTTING INSTRUCTIONS

White: Cut center square 10" x 10". (Trim to 6½" x 6½" after embroidery.)

Cut 2 strips 1½" x width of fabric, then cut into 3 rectangles 1½" x 13" for Nine-Patches.

Cut 1 strip 2½" x width of fabric, then cut 4 rectangles 2½" x 6½".

Cut 2 strips 2" x 12½" for side borders.

Cut 2 strips 2" x 15½" for top and bottom borders.

Red: Cut 2 strips 1½" x width of fabric, then cut into 3 rectangles 1½" x 13" and 4 rectangles 1½" x 6½".

Backing: Cut 1 square 15½" x 15½".

CONSTRUCTION

1. Sew 1 white 1½" x 13" rectangle to each side of 1 red 1½" x 13" rectangle. Press seams toward red. Crosscut into 8 units 1½" x 3½".

2. Stitch 1 red 1½" x 13" rectangle to each side of 1 white 1½" x 13" rectangle. Press seams toward red. Crosscut into 4 units 1½" x 3½".

3. Assemble 4 Nine-Patch blocks as shown on page 30.

4. Sew 1 red rectangle 1½" x 6½" to 1 white rectangle 2½" x 6½". Press seams toward red. Make 4.

5. Assemble 1 Puss in the Corner block as shown on page 31.

6. Sew 1 white 2" x 12½" border to each side of block. Sew 1 white 2" x 15½" border to top and bottom of block.

7. If desired, baste piping around outside edge of block, clipping at each corner. Overlap ends of piping and baste raw edges into the seam. Stitch backing to pillow top, right sides together, leaving opening for inserting pillow form. Insert and close the opening using a slipstitch.

Chapter Three

BOUNTIFUL AUTUMN!

Things to share with friends…

Decorate or carve pumpkins to welcome trick-or-treaters. Children make friends naturally, and we can always use a few more "children" friends in our lives!

If a friend has pumpkins growing, sneak into her patch early in the season when she is gone and scratch the names of her kids or grandchildren on the pumpkins while they are still green. As the pumpkins grow and ripen, so do the names.

Decorate a special pumpkin and leave it at your friend's front door. Be sure to add button eyes and a fat quarter scarf. Don't tell her you did it, and let her wonder who cares that much about her.

Gather leaves from under a tree dressed in their autumn colors. Press them in a heavy book between two sheets of paper. After a few weeks, remove them from the book, tie the stems with a tiny bow, and place the pressed leaves in a pretty frame for that special friend!

Autumn is a second spring when every leaf's a flower.

Albert Camus

WHEN THE FROST IS ON THE PUMPKIN

Finished quilt size: 58" x 58". Quilted by Lynne Todoroff.

Have you ever seen so many pumpkins on one quilt? This quilt lends itself to any method of appliqué. We chose the spray starch method and then machine blanket stitched, but you could hand appliqué or use fusible webbing. This quilt would also be wonderful made on a black wool background. Use assorted gold, yellow, and cream wool for the pumpkins.

MATERIALS

2¹/₂ yards for background

¹/₄ yard each of 12 or 18 assorted prints for pumpkins

¹/₈ yard for pumpkin stems

¹/₄ yard leaf fabric

¹/₃ yard for inner border

1 yard for outer border

¹/₂ yard for binding

3³/₄ yards for backing

62" x 62" batting

1 skein brown DMC embroidery floss

CUTTING INSTRUCTIONS

Background fabric: Cut 9 strips 9" x width of fabric, then cut into 36 squares 9" x 9". (They will be trimmed to 8¹/₂" x 8¹/₂" squares after appliqué.)

Inner border fabric: Cut and piece 3 strips, 1¹/₂" x width of fabric, from this cut 2 side border strips 1¹/₂" x 48¹/₂".

Cut and piece 3 strips, 1¹/₂" x width of fabric, then cut 2 strips 1¹/₂" x 50¹/₂" for top and bottom borders.

Outer border fabric: Cut and piece 3 strips, 4¹/₂" x width of fabric, then cut 2 side border strips 4¹/₂" x 50¹/₂".

Cut and piece 3 strips, 4¹/₂" x width of fabric, then cut 2 strips 4¹/₂" x 58¹/₂" for top and bottom borders.

Appliqué fabrics: Cut out shapes for your favorite method of appliqué (see General Instructions, pages 5–8), using the patterns on the pullout.

Cut out 36 pumpkins and stems (12 of each) and 12 leaves.

Binding: Cut 7 strips 2¹/₄ x width of fabric.

NOW LET'S SEW!

1. Using your favorite method (see General Instructions, pages 5–8), appliqué pumpkins and stems to center of each block. We used the spray-starched method and a machine blanket stitch.

2. After completing appliqué, embroider lines on pumpkin using 2 strands of embroidery floss and outline stitch. If you prefer, you can quilt in the lines on the pumpkins later. (The leaves are added after blocks are stitched together.)

3. Trim blocks to 8¹/₂" x 8¹/₂".

ASSEMBLE THE QUILT

1. Stitch the blocks together in rows referring to the diagram and color photograph. Join row 1 to row 2, row 2 to row 3, and so on. Press the top.

2. Appliqué the leaves to the pumpkin blocks, following the photograph. Embroider random vines and tendrils as desired.

3. Add the inner borders (sides, then top and bottom).

4. Add the outer borders (sides, then top and bottom).

5. You are now ready to layer and baste your quilt (see General Instructions, page 10).

6. Quilt as desired.

7. Bind your quilt (see General Instructions, pages 10–11).

When the Frost is on the Pumpkin Assembly

AUTUMN LEAVES

Finished quilt size: 41½" x 48½". Quilted by Lynne Todoroff.

We've designed this basket quilt for autumn, but you could use it for any season of the year. Place running rabbits around the basket for an Easter quilt or holly leaves for Christmas. The possibilities are unlimited!

MATERIALS

1⅔ yards cream for center background, corner blocks and borders

3 fat quarters (light, medium, and dark) for basket

⅛ yard each of 4 fabrics for oak leaves

⅛ yard for vine leaves

1 fat quarter for berries

1 fat quarter for bias stems

10" x 10" for birds

5" x 5" for bird wings

1⅓ yards gold for border and binding

1⅔ yards of 45" to 54" fabric, turned horizontally for backing

DMC embroidery floss brown # 433

Water-erasable fabric marker

¼" bias maker or bias bar

46" x 53" batting

CUTTING INSTRUCTIONS

Cream: Cut 1 rectangle 32" x 39" for center.

Cut 4 strips 1½" x 39" and 4 strips 1½" x 32" for border.

Cut 4 squares 5½" x 5½" for corners.

Gold: Cut 6 strips 1½" x 39" and 6 strips 1½" x 32" for the border.

Cut 6 strips 2¼" x width of fabric for binding.

Bias stem fat quarter: Cut 3 bias strips ½" x 23".

Appliqué fabrics: Cut out shapes for your favorite method of appliqué (see General Instructions, pages 5–8), using the patterns on page 39. **All patterns must be enlarged 220%.**

 ## NOW LETS SEW!
Appliqué

1. Follow the instructions for needle-turn appliqué (see General Instructions, pages 5–6). Fold the background fabric in half both horizontally and vertically. Match the dotted lines of the basket pattern onto the fold lines of the background. Glue and pin the entire basket in place before you begin to appliqué.

2. Appliqué the basket's handle first, and then, starting with the top layers of scallops, appliqué the basket. Leave 2 openings on the center section of the basket top (as indicated on pattern) to insert the bias vines. These will be stitched closed after the vines are appliquéd.

3. Following the General Instructions on page 8, make 3 bias vines ¼" x 23".

4. Insert the ends of 2 vines approximately ¼" into the basket top. Following color photo, glue and pin vines in place on each side of the basket. Glue and pin remaining vine in place at the top center of the background square. Appliqué vines in place.

5. Following the color photo, appliqué the 22 vine leaves and 13 berries to the vines, and one of the birds above the right-hand side of the top vine. Leave tip of 1 vine leaf free until top border is added. Following photo, appliqué the second bird (reversed) to the center of the basket.

6. Appliqué 15 oak leaves to the center background square as in the photo. (Stem embroidery is done after quilting is completed.) Appliqué 1 leaf onto each of the corner squares.

Pieced Borders

1. Stitch together side borders following the diagram. Spray seam lightly with spray starch before pressing. Press the seam toward gold after each strip is added. Remember to stitch seams in opposite directions (see General Instructions, page 5). This will help keep your border from "waving." Sew side borders to quilt.

2. Repeat Step 1 for top and bottom borders. Sew a corner square to each end of the top and bottom borders. Make sure leaves are pointing in the direction shown in the color photo. Press the seams toward the border. Sew top and bottom borders to quilt.

ASSEMBLE THE QUILT

1. You are now ready to layer and baste (see General Instructions, page 10).

2. Quilt as desired.

3. Use 3 strands of light brown DMC thread to embroider stems using an outline stitch. Refer to photo for the directions of the stems.

4. Bind your quilt (see General Instructions, pages 10–11).

Love is blind; friendship closes its eyes.

Old Proverb

Autumn Leaves Assembly

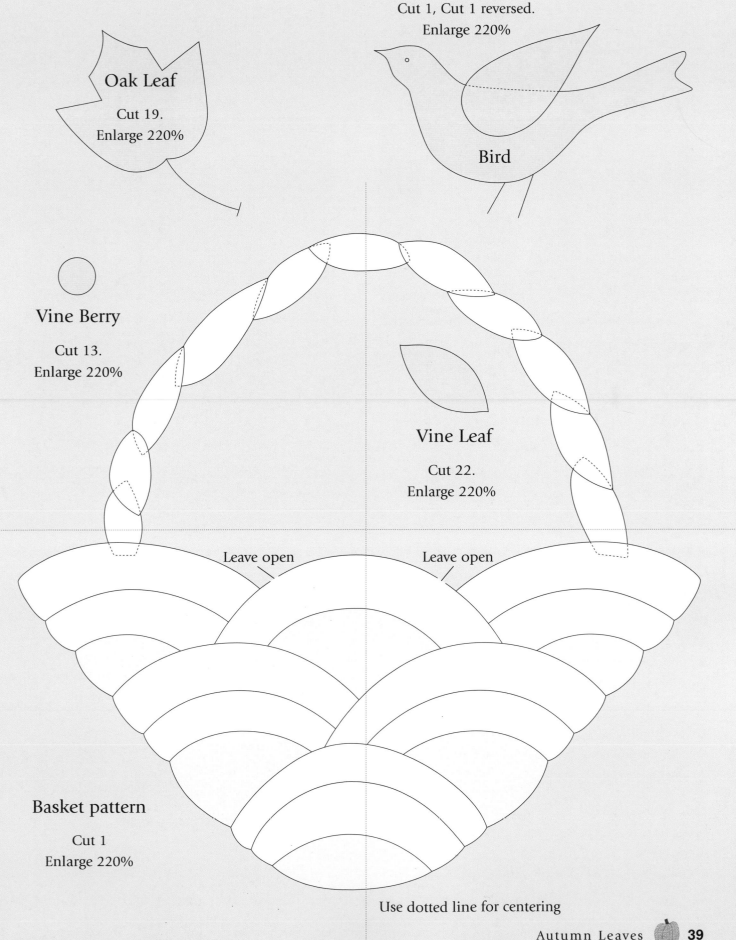

Oak Leaf

Cut 19.
Enlarge 220%

Cut 1, Cut 1 reversed.
Enlarge 220%

Bird

Vine Berry

Cut 13.
Enlarge 220%

Vine Leaf

Cut 22.
Enlarge 220%

Leave open

Leave open

Basket pattern

Cut 1
Enlarge 220%

Use dotted line for centering

PUMPKIN PILLOW

REVERSIBLE COASTERS

Finished pillow size: 9½" x 9½"

Finished coaster size: 4" x 4"

 ## MATERIALS

2 squares 11" x 11" wool or wool felt for top and backing

8" x 8" wool or wool felt for pumpkin

3" x 3" wool or wool felt for stem

3" x 3" wool or wool felt for leaf

Four 1" buttons for corners of pillow

1 skein brown DMC embroidery floss

1 bag stuffing

CONSTRUCTION

1. Trace your favorite pumpkin pattern onto freezer paper. Iron to selected fabric and cut out on traced line.

2. Using a hand blanket stitch, appliqué pumpkin and stem to background (see page 9). Embroider vine using 2 strands of floss and outline stitch. Secure leaf to end of vine using a running stitch in the center (the edges are not stitched down).

3. Trim the pillow top and backing squares to 9½" x 9½".

4. Stitch by machine around pillow 1" from outer edge, leaving a 2"-wide opening for stuffing. Stuff pillow and machine stitch opening closed. Sew a button to each corner.

MATERIALS FOR ONE COASTER

2 squares 4" x 4" wool or wool felt for background

Scraps of wool or wool felt for pumpkin, stem, and leaf

1 skein brown DMC embroidery floss

1 skein DMC embroidery floss in matching or contrasting color to background fabric (for outside edge)

CONSTRUCTION

1. Cut 2 pieces wool or wool felt 4" x 4".

2. Trace 1 leaf (oak leaf pattern on page 39) onto freezer paper. Iron to selected felt and cut out on traced line. Trace 1 pumpkin and small leaf pattern onto freezer paper. Iron to selected fabric and cut out on traced line.

3. Hand or machine blanket stitch felt pieces to background square, following photo. Place background squares right sides together and hand blanket stitch around the coaster.

4. Repeat steps 1–3 for desired number of coasters.

Chapter Four

WONDERFUL WINTER!

The holidays are a time to start a new tradition to share with your friends. We celebrate our birthdays and Christmas each year with Barbara Brown. On the appointed day, we get together for lunch and do a craft of some kind. One year we painted snowmen faces on white Christmas balls to put away for gifts.

Do a gift exchange with your quilter friends. Draw names in advance. Each person has to bring a gift that is "old" and related to quilting (jars to store buttons, tins to store pins, or—if you are lucky— old quilt squares). You never know what surprises people can find at antique stores or flea markets. We guarantee there will be laughter and fun.

. . . And for any season of the year from Margaret:

For a friend who is shut in, gather all of your catalogs and place in a basket tied with a pretty bow. Include a picnic lunch. Spread a quilt on the bed and have a picnic. When you leave, she will love looking at all those catalogs. I know because a friend did this for me. Thank you, Marylee Post!

One time in my life I was fortunate to have a dear friend, Marilyn Benson, who lived next door. Every other afternoon, she would take my four kids at 4 p.m. and keep them at her house while I took a bubble bath and relaxed for an hour. The next day I did the same thing for her. We did this every Monday through Friday until I moved away. How I miss her.

Friendship is like a Christmas tree, decorated with warm memories and shared joys. You're the slightly cracked ornament that always makes me smile.

Author unknown

★IT'S CHRISTMAS TIME IN THE COUNTRY

We've created a Christmas quilt that looks good in any fabric using any type of appliqué method! We've shown it both in cotton fabric and wool felt. Need a gift for that special friend? Choose one of the 12" squares and make a pillow. Appliqué the holly and berries to our little stocking pattern, and you have the perfect napkin holder. Or, make some placemats for your holiday table, and your family will feel very special!

Cotton Version. Finished quilt size: 39" x 56"

Wool Felt Version.

MATERIALS

If doing a wool version, preshrink wool by wetting with water. Gently squeeze out excess water (do not twist). Place in dryer until almost dry. Lay flat to continue drying. Note: all seams on wool felt version are pressed open. Add ¼ yard to all yardage if you need to preshrink the wool. All wool appliqués are blanket stitched.

Background Fabrics for cotton:

½ yard for house block

½ yard for holly wreath and candle wreath blocks

½ yard for tree and star bouquet blocks

⅝ yard for side borders

⅓ yard for top border

¼ yard for corner squares

¼ yard for bottom border

Background Fabric for wool: 3½ yards felt or wool

Appliqué Fabrics:

House block: 1 fat quarter for heart, 1 fat quarter for leaves and stem, 9" x 5" for house, 3" x 8" for roof, 3" x 3" for chimneys, 3" x 3" for flower, 3" x 3" for windows, 3" x 3" for door

Holly wreath block: 1 fat quarter for leaves and bias strip, 9" x 5" for berries

Candle wreath block: 1 fat quarter for leaves and bias strip, 8" x 4" for candle holder, 2" x 3" for candle, 2" x 2" for flame, 9" x 9" for flowers, 5" x 5" for flower centers

Tree block: 1 fat quarter for tree fabric

Star bouquet block: 1 fat quarter for bias strips and leaves, 1 fat quarter for stars

Side borders: ¼ yard for trees, 1 fat quarter for stars, 4" x 6" for tree trunks

½ yard for vines and leaves

⅛ yard for berries

⅓ yard for sashing

Finishing for cotton version:

½ yard for binding

2½ yards backing

43" x 60" batting

1 skein DMC embroidery floss # 814

¼" and ⅜" bias makers or bias bars

Roxanne's Glue-Baste-It

29 buttons (¼") for tree block (see Resources, page 56)

Water-erasable marker or General's marking pencil

Finishing for wool version:

DMC floss or wool floss to match or contrast with each fabric ¼ yard wool felt for outside border strips

Five ¾" buttons for tops of tabs

CUTTING INSTRUCTIONS

Background Fabrics:

Cut 1 rectangle 25½" x 16½" for house block.

Cut 2 strips 6½" x width of fabric, then cut into 8 squares 6½" x 6½", for holly wreath/candle wreath backgrounds if using a stripe. If using single background piece, cut 2 squares 12½" x 12½".

Cut 2 squares 12½" x 12½" for tree and star bouquet blocks.

Cut 2 strips 6½" x 42½" for side borders.

Cut 1 rectangle 8½" x 25½" for top border.

Cut 2 rectangles 6½" x 8½" for corner squares.

Cut 1 strip 4½" x 39½" for bottom border.

Appliqué Fabrics:

Cut out shapes for your favorite method of appliqué using the patterns on pullout. Patterns have not been reversed.

Sashing and binding:

Cut 7 strips 1½" x width of fabric, then cut into 2 strips 42½" x 1½", 2 strips 1½" x 39½", 2 strips 1½" x 25½", 2 rectangles 1½" x 12½", and 2 strips 8½" x 1½" for sashing.

For cotton version, cut 6 strips 2¼" x width of the fabric for the binding.

For wool version, cut 2 strips 1½" x 56" for side outside borders, and 2 strips 1½" x 40" for top and bottom outside borders. Cut 5 tabs 1½" x 8".

NOW LET'S SEW!

Fold each block in half vertically and horizontally to find the center. Following the photograph, appliqué pieces on each block using the method of your choice. We used the needle-turn method (see General Instructions, pages 5–6) on the cotton version. We used hand blanket stitch on the wool version.

1. House block: Appliqué the large heart to background fabric. Appliqué the house according to the numbers on the pattern. For cotton version, make a bias strip ⅜" x 15½" (see General Instructions, page 8). For wool version, trace stem pattern. Appliqué the stem, flower, and leaves to the heart (hide raw edge of stem under heart).

2. Holly wreath block: If using a striped background, alternate the direction of the stripes and stitch top 2 sections together, following direction of stripe in color photo. Press seam to left. Stitch bottom 2 sections together and press seam to right. Stitch top section to bottom section. Press.

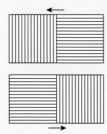

For cotton version, make a bias strip ⅜" x 13½" for center circle. Using a water erasable marker or marking pencil, trace the circle pattern onto the center of your background fabric. Appliqué the bias strip to the background over the traced lines, overlapping ¼" where edges meet. Trim, if necessary. Place block and pattern over light box or window and trace "Joy" onto fabric using water erasable marker or marking pencil. Embroider "Joy" using outline stitch (see General Instructions, page 9) and 3 strands of floss. Appliqué holly leaves, using the pattern for placement. Appliqué berries as desired.

For wool version, trace circle pattern from pullout onto freezer paper, cut out on traced lines and blanketstitch in place. Then attach leaves wtih a running stitch down center and attach berries with a cross stitch with french knots in the center.

3. Candle wreath block: If using stripes, follow sewing directions for holly wreath background, step 2. Appliqué the candle holder to the center of the background square. Make a bias strip ¼" x 29½" (see General Instructions, page 8). Using a water erasable marker or marking pencil, trace the circle pattern to background fabric. On cotton version, appliqué bias strip to the background, forming a circle. On wool version, embroider circle with an outline stitch following pullout. Appliqué flowers, flower centers, and leaves.

4. Tree block: Appliqué the tree to the background. Buttons are added after quilting on the cotton version. For wool version, appliqué 14 pears and 2 birds.

5. Star bouquet block: Make ⅜" bias strips (see General Instructions, page 8) for cotton version. For wool, cut ⅜" strips. For cotton and wool, make one 10" strip for center stem, one 11" strip for curved bottom stem, and two 5" strips for side stems. Pin and glue center stem in place. Pin and glue side stems in place, being sure to place the ends under the center stem. Pin and glue bottom curved stem in place. Appliqué all stems. Appliqué stars and leaves in place, following color photo.

6. Side borders: Appliqué 3 stars, 2 tree trunks, and 2 trees to each side border, following the photo.

7. Top bird border: Make a bias strip ¼" x 22½" (see General Instructions, page 8) and appliqué to background following the color photo for cotton version. For wool, draw a curving line and embroider with outline stitch. Appliqué bird, small holly leaves, and small holly berries in place as desired.

8. Corner squares: Appliqué large holly leaves and berries to background squares, making sure the leaves face in opposite directions. For wool, attach berries with cross stitch and French knot in center.

9. Bottom border: For cotton version, make a bias strip ¼" x 39" for vine (see General Instructions, page 8). Appliqué to the background fabric, following color photo. For wool version, embroider vine using an outline stitch. Appliqué small leaves and small holly berries in place, as desired.

ASSEMBLE THE QUILT

1. Following the diagram below, sew the top bird border, sashing strips, and corner blocks together. Press (on wool version, press all seams open). Sew the 39½" sashing strip to the bottom of this section. Press.

2. Following the diagram, assemble the center section of the quilt. Sew the sashing strips and side tree borders to this section. Sew to the section from step 1. Press.

3. Following the diagram, sew the 39½" sashing strip to the bottom holly border. Sew to the bottom of the quilt. Press.

Cotton-Version Finishing

1. It's time to layer and baste your quilt (see General Instructions, page 10) for cotton version.

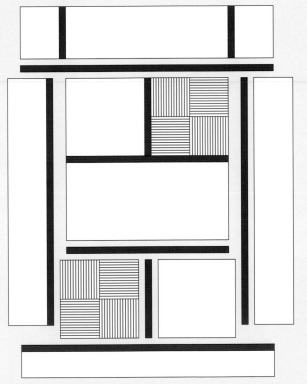

It's Christmas Time in the Country Assembly

2. Quilt as desired.

3. Following the photo, stitch the buttons to the tree block.

4. Bind your quilt (see General Instructions, pages 10–11).

Wool-Version Finishing

1. Add the side border strips. With pinking shears or a pinking rotary cutter, trim long edge of all 4 border strips. Be very careful to cut a straight line and to trim just along the edge, leaving as much border as possible. Pin the 2 side border strips to the quilt top, overlapping quilt top and border strip ⅜" and facing the pinked edge to the outside. Sew in place ¼" from side edge of quilt top. Repeat for top and bottom borders.

2. With pinking shears or pinking rotary cutter, trim 1 end of each tab strip to a point. Pin tabs to back of quilt top, making sure the pinked edge extends up. Space the tabs 1" from sides of quilt top and approximately 7¾" apart. Stitch tabs in place. Fold tabs to front of quilt and pin in place. Attach tabs to quilt top with ¾" buttons.

3. Our wool quilt does *not* have any backing, batting, or quilting. Hang it from a brass or painted wood curtain rod with finials on the end. For the lodge look, hang it on a branch cut from a tree.

 When using freezer paper, you do not have to trace all of the holly leaves because you can peel the paper off the wool and use it time and time again. Trace only 4 or 5 small holly leaves and 1 of the large holly leaves. Repeat for the flowers, stars, and side trees.

PLACEMATS
AUTUMN/WINTER

Finished placemat size: 19" x 15"

 ## PLACEMAT MATERIALS

½ yard each of 2 contrasting colors of wool or wool felt for each placemat

Scraps of wool or wool felt for selected designs

DMC embroidery floss to match selected fabrics

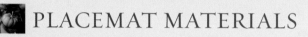 ## PLACEMAT CONSTRUCTION

1. Cut 1 piece of wool or wool felt 16" x 20" for each side of placemat. Trim to 15" x 19" after appliqué.

2. Trace appliqué patterns (on pullout) onto freezer paper and iron to selected pieces of felt. Autumn uses 2 leaves. Winter uses 5 small holly leaves and 8 small berries. Cut out felt on pattern lines and remove freezer paper.

3. Following the color photo, blanket stitch the stem to the background before attaching pumpkin to placemat. Leave the top edge of the pumpkin open for your favorite napkin. Join the leaves on the Autumn mat using 2 strands of floss and an outline stitch. Attach the berries on the Winter mat using a cross stitch and a French knot in the center.

4. With wrong sides together, join Autumn and Winter with a blanket stitch.

STOCKING
NAPKIN HOLDER

Finished placemat size: 19" x 15"

Finished stocking size: 7" x 10"

 ## STOCKING MATERIALS

2 felt rectangles 8½" x 12"

8" x 8" red felt

6" x 6" green felt

3 buttons

Scalloped pinking shears (optional)

STOCKING CONSTRUCTION

1. Trace patterns onto freezer paper. Iron patterns to felt and cut out on traced lines.

2. Appliqué small leaves to stocking front with a running stitch down the center, leaving the edges free. Sew 3 buttons for berries. Pin heel, toe, and scalloped top to front of stocking, following the photo.

3. With wrong sides together, stitch around stocking, using ¼" seam and leaving top open. If desired, trim edges with scalloped pinking shears.

SNOWMEN WARM
YOUR HEART AND FEET

Finished quilt size: 44" x 56". Quilted by Lynne Todoroff.

This quilt just makes you feel happy! Add a flannel backing and curl up in front
of the fire with a hot cup of cocoa. If you are not up to a full-size quilt, pick
your favorite snowmen and you have a darling wall hanging.

MATERIALS

½ yard each of 2 different fabrics for the Four-Patches

2¼ yards for background of snowmen and outer border

1½ yards total assorted whites for snowmen

1 fat quarter for trees

Assorted scraps for snowmen details

3 yards light fusible webbing

1 skein each of the following DMC 6 strand embroidery floss: blanc, black #310, gold #783, green #904 and #937, red #321, orange #3853, and yellow #677 and #726

2 skeins brown #898

Fabric marking pencil

¾ yard for binding and inner border

2¾ yards backing if piecing horizontally; use 3½ yards of piecing vertically.

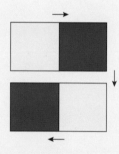

48" x 60" batting

CUTTING INSTRUCTIONS

Cut 4 strips 3½" x width of fabric from each Four-Patch fabric.

Cut 5 strips 7" x width of fabric, then cut into 21 squares 7" x 7" for snowman backgrounds. (They will be trimmed to 6½" x 6½" squares after appliqué.)

Cut 2 strips 1½" x 42½" for side inner borders and 2 strips 1½" x 32½" for top and bottom inner borders.

Cut and piece 3 strips 7"-width of fabric, then cut 2 strips 7" x 44½" for side outer borders.

Cut 2 strips 7" x 32½" for top and bottom outer borders.

Cut 6 strips 2¼" x width of fabric for binding.

NOW LETS SEW!
Four-Patch Blocks

1. Sew the Four-Patch fabric strips together in pairs. Press seams toward the darker fabric. Crosscut into 36 units 3½" x 6½".

2. Assemble 18 Four-Patch blocks. Press seams in direction of arrows.

3. Following General Instructions for fusible webbing appliqué (see pages 6–7), trace then fuse all 17 snowmen blocks and 4 corner tree blocks. (Patterns are already reversed for tracing.)

4. Blanket stitch by hand or machine around snowmen. Trace arms, noses, and details onto snowmen blocks. All embroidery uses 2 strands of floss. Satin stitch noses, outline stitch arms and other detail, and eyes and mouth are French knots unless noted on pattern. Trim blocks to 6½" x 6½".

A friend is like a quilt, designed by heart, pieced in time, sewn by hand and bound to keep you covered.

Author unknown

ASSEMBLE THE QUILT

1. Sew the blocks by rows, alternating snowman blocks and Four-Patch blocks. Press the top.

2. Following color photo trace and then fuse 22 sets of snowmen to the borders . Place snowmen on border, working from center to outside edge. They are approximately 1" apart and ¾" from bottom edge. Be sure to allow for seam allowance at each end of all borders. Blanket stitch by hand or machine around each snowman.

3. Trace arms and noses onto snowmen and embroider with 2 strands of floss. Use outline stitch for arms and satin stitch for noses. After the snowmen are stitched, trim borders to 6½" wide.

4. Sew inner borders to quilt (sides, then top and bottom). Press toward the border.

5. Sew side outer borders to quilt. Press toward the inner border.

6. Sew 1 Tree block to each end of the top and bottom borders. Press toward block.

7. Sew top and bottom outer borders to quilt. Press toward inner border.

8. You are now ready to layer and baste your quilt (see General Instructions, page 10). Fix yourself a cup of hot chocolate and relax! You are now a gold-medal winner for blanket stitching!

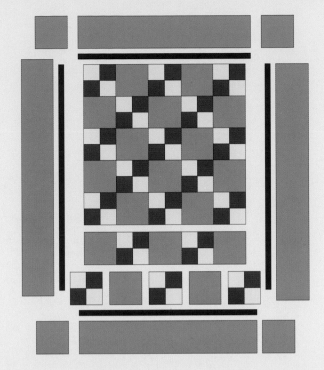

Snowmen Warm Your Heart and Feet Assembly

9. Quilt as desired.

10. Bind your quilt (see General Instructions, pages 10–11).

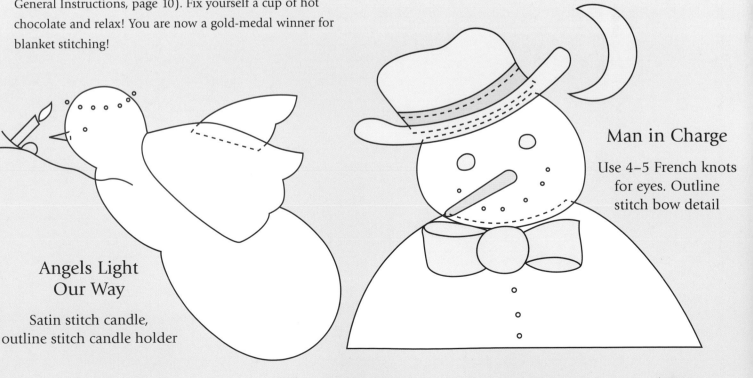

Angels Light Our Way

Satin stitch candle, outline stitch candle holder

Man in Charge

Use 4–5 French knots for eyes. Outline stitch bow detail

Momma's Boy

Straight stitch
stars French knot
ends of stars

Sweet Dreams

Outline stitch eye

Star Bright

*Note: Small snowflakes
belong to Away We Go*

Away We Go

Straight stitch small stars.

*Note: Large star belongs
to Star Bright*

I'll Diet When
the Snow Melts

From My Heart

Satin stitch star and
appliqué heart

Border Girls

Catch a
Falling Star

Angel Baby

For the Birds

Batter Up

Martha

Satin stitch hearts
and stars

Friends are lights in winter;
the older the friend, the
brighter the light.

Roger Roseblatt

Shopper Girl

Here Bunny Bunny

Work Until
You Melt

Love Never Melts

Trace hat all as one. Trace hat ribbon
and flower separately.

HOLIDAY GIFT BAG

Finished gift bag size: 8" x 10½"

CONSTRUCTION

1. Trace your favorite snowman onto freezer paper, iron to felt, and cut out on traced line. Remove freezer paper.

2. Embroider details on snowman and glue to background felt.

3. Cut felt background to 6" x 8". Trim edges with pinking shears.

Glue to bag and embellish as desired.

For larger bags, enlarge pattern to fit.

Give a snowman to a friend and Christmas will be merrier!

MATERIALS

8" x 10½" gift bag

Felt scraps at least 7" x 9" for snowman and background

Embroidery floss

Glue

Embellishments

RESOURCES

CRAFTS 4 ME

P.O. Box 1716

Discovery Bay, CA 94514

Phone: 1-800-917-7888

Email: contactus@crafts4me.com

Web: www.crafts4me.com

Tiny ¼" buttons and Bunny Hill Designs patterns

ROXANNE'S GLUE-BASTE-IT:

Roxanne International

295 West Louise Avenue

Manteca, CA 95336

Phone: 1-800-993-4445

Web: www.thatperfectstitch.com

COTTON PATCH MAIL ORDER

3405 Hall Lane, Dept, CTB

Lafayette, CA 94549

Phone: 1-800-835-4418

Email: quiltusa@yahoo.com

Web: www.quiltusa.com

Appliqué pressing sheet and other quilting supplies

Dealer of machine embroidery cards Bernina's

"United we Stand" and "Redwork for Children."

A friend is better than chocolate ice cream, maybe a friend is somebody you give up the last cookie for.

Telly, Sesame Street

ABOUT THE AUTHORS

Anne Sutton and Margaret Peters

MARGARET PETERS

Starting out in the quilting world as a quilt representative selling quilting supplies, Margaret never dreamed she would be writing a third book; nor did she imagine she would be featured in other publications, lecture all over the United States, and appear on such TV programs as *Simply Quilts* and the *Carol Duval Show*. She is also a featured quilter in Jean Wells' *Through the Garden Gate*. Numerous quilting books have been photographed at Margaret's home (including parts of this book), and her home was featured in *American Patchwork and Quilting* (December 2003).

Margaret has always believed people should reach for the stars. She warns, however, when you do take hold of your star, be prepared for a journey of incredible experiences. What a joyful trip this has been for her.

Margaret's other patterns are available at MandP53@aol.com.

ANNE SUTTON

When Anne Sutton signed up for a blanket stitch class from Margaret Peters, she had no idea it would change her life forever! It was the beginning of a new friendship and a new career. Anne has been quilting for only seven years, but sewing, which she has done since the age of eight, has always been a passion. She was the director of catering at a four-star hotel for many years, and yet she continued to sew every chance she had. She loves that she can finally put her courses to good use!

Anne has been featured in *Garden-Inspired Quilts* by Jean and Valori Wells, and *American Patchwork and Quilting Magazine* (December 2003). She also completed a program in fashion design with training in sewing techniques, pattern drafting, fabric, and color study. Her 20-pound cat named Mr. Paws has also had a full-page spread in *American Patchwork and Quilting Magazine* (June 2003), but so far he hasn't taken up quilting. Anne designs under the name of "Bunny Hill Designs."